Ripley's Believe It or Not!®

Developed and produced by Ripley Publishing Ltd

This edition published and distributed by:

 Mason Crest
450 Parkway Drive, Suite D, Broomall, PA 19008
www.masoncrest.com

J031.02 / Rip

Printed and bound in the United States of America

First printing
9 8 7 6 5 4 3 2 1

02|15

Ripley's Believe It or Not!
Remarkable Feats
ISBN: 978-1-4222-3152-4 (hardback)
Ripley's Believe It or Not!—Complete 8 Title Series
ISBN: 978-1-4222-3147-0

Cataloging-in-Publication Data on file with the Library of Congress

3 5991 00091 1569

PUBLISHER'S NOTE
While every effort has been made to verify the accuracy of the entries in this book, the
Publishers cannot be held responsible for any errors contained in the work. They would
be glad to receive any information from readers.

WARNING
Some of the stunts and activities in this book are undertaken by experts and should not
be attempted by anyone without adequate training and supervision.

Ripley's Believe It or Not!®

Download The Weird

REMARKABLE FEATS

www.MasonCrest.com

REMARKABLE FEATS

Amazing achievements. Open up your
eyes to these extraordinary exploits.
Look out for the surfer who rode a
90-ft (27-m) wave, the grandmother
who is also a bodybuilder, and
the incredible Lizardman!

Strongman Kevin Fast and his son, Jacob,
pulled two fire trucks 100 ft (30 m) down
the street...

Louis Cole from London, England, has an appetite that defies belief. The daring digester has eaten some of the most disgusting things imaginable for his Internet videos, including 21 live locusts, over 600 wriggling mealworms in one sitting, and one very large and active scorpion—the creature's stinger was sensibly left on the plate. Clearly not one to back down from a challenge, Louis has forced down every freaky foodstuff suggested to him, from hissing cockroaches to a hairy tarantula, and he has never vomited anything back up.

LOCUST COUNT: 17

Super Stomach

Louis Cole's
Monstrous Menu

- LIVE MAY BUG
- LIVE HOUSE SPIDER
- 21 LIVE LOCUSTS
- RAW SHEEP BRAIN
- ENTIRE BOTTLE OF WASABI SAUCE
- 3 LIVE COCKROACHES
- 10 MICE LIQUEFIED IN A BLENDER
- DECOMPOSING FROG
- LIVE GIANT SCORPION
- 660 LIVE MEALWORMS
- LIVE WASP

LOCUST COUNT: 21

MEALWORM COUNT: 660

Ripley's ask

How did you start extreme eating? I can't remember how I got into extreme eating, but I know I've always been interested in trying new things and challenging the norm. The show started when me and some friends decided to share some amusing videos of me eating bugs.

What has been your least favorite eating challenge? I think the cockroaches were my least favorite, as they tasted vile and were wiggling and hissing in my mouth while I was chewing, an all-round horrendous ordeal. (I think you can tell by my expressions in the video!)

Has your freaky eating ever made you ill? I've never been ill from the live meals, but I once got a dodgy stomach from eating raw sheep brains.

WHAT A MOUTHFUL!

On July 4, 2011, Dinesh Shivnath Upadhyaya, a teacher from Mumbai, India, set a new world record by fitting 800 drinking straws into his mouth at the same time and keeping them there for 30 seconds.

800 straws!

92 pencils!

R BOTTLE-CAP CHAIN Students and teachers at Seaview Elementary School in Linwood, New Jersey, created a chain from 10,714 bottle caps.

R CANADIAN CROSSING In 2011, Kevin Robins of Fort McMurray, Alberta, Canada, cycled across Canada from Vancouver, British Columbia, to St. John's, Newfoundland, in just over 22 days, beating the previous record by a day and a half. He covered a total of 4,500 mi (7,200 km), clocking up an average pace of 200 mi (323 km) a day.

R LARGEST KILT Ordering 170 sq yd (142 sq m) of material, Steve Campbell, a Scotsman living in the United States, made the world's largest kilt and used it to dress the 80-ft-tall (24-m) *Golden Driller* statue in Tulsa, Oklahoma, for the 2011 Oklahoma Scottish Festival. The supersized kilt was 25 ft (7.6 m) long and had a waist measuring 48 ft (14.6 m), nearly 14 times bigger than a U.S. extra-large size.

MOUTHWATERING RECORDS

• 800 DRINKING STRAWS	Dinesh Upadhyaya (India)
• 159 CIGARETTES	Jim Mouth (United States)
• 109 LIVE BEES	Dr. Norman Gary (United States)
• 92 PENCILS	Dinesh Upadhyaya (India)
• 57 GRAPES	Shobhit Keshvdass (India)
• 41 CIGARS	Jim Mouth (United States)
• 22 LIVE SCORPIONS	Maged Almalki (Saudi Arabia)
• 11 LIVE RATTLESNAKES	Jackie Bibby (United States)
• 11 LIVE COCKROACHES	Travis Fessler (United States)
• 5 TENNIS BALLS	Augie the dog (United States)

Walking on Water

Polish kiteboarder Maciek Kozierski temporarily defied the laws of physics by walking on water—on Israel's Sea of Galilee where Jesus is said to have walked on water in the New Testament. After more than 50 unsuccessful attempts in awkward wind conditions over four days, Kozierski finally used his kite to accelerate to maximum speed, then let go of the kite and ran off his board so that he was miraculously walking on water for a few steps.

WONDER WHEEL On June 18, 2011, the Lilly fireworks factory in Mqabba, Malta, lit the world's biggest pinwheel (Catherine Wheel) firework. With a diameter of 105 ft (32 m), it was 45 times the size of the average car wheel.

ARMY MEDIC At 76 years old, U.S. Army medic Dr. John Burson, an ear, nose, and throat specialist from Villa Rica, Georgia, was posted to Afghanistan to take his fourth tour of duty in war zones since 2005.

UNDERWATER ESCAPE U.S. entertainer Thomas Blacke escaped from a pair of handcuffs underwater in a world record time of 8.34 seconds on October 27, 2010, in Yarmouth, Massachusetts.

WILD WALK In windy conditions in August 2011, Austrian daredevil Michael Kemeter completed a death-defying walk for 148 ft (45 m) along a ¾-in-wide (2-cm) slackline at an altitude of 2,600 ft (793 m) on Austria's highest mountain, the Grossglockner. He had a safety rope but wore no shoes and despite the cold went topless to reduce wind resistance. A week earlier, he crossed a 525-ft-long (160-m) slackline—the longest in the world—over the Gruenen See in Styria, Austria. In slacklining, the thin nylon line is anchored between two points, but unlike a tightrope it is not taut and is allowed to sway around in the air.

SOLO PILOT On June 4, 2011, nine-year-old Bobby Bradley of Albuquerque, New Mexico, became the youngest solo hot-air balloon pilot when he flew a balloon for 26 minutes over his home state before making a perfect landing. Bobby already had 30 hours' flying experience with his parents—both keen balloonists—and started taking control of the burner when he was just four.

DEEP BREATH On August 5, 2011, pool supervisor Joe Wilkie of Tonawanda, New York, walked a record 241 ft 6 in (73.6 m) underwater on a single breath in 1 minute 15 seconds while carrying a 25-lb (11.3-kg) weight to hold him down.

CARTON REGATTA Thirty-six teams used 45,000 empty milk cartons to make rowboats to take part in the 2011 milk carton boat regatta over a 165-ft-long (50-m) course on Latvia's Lielupe River.

POGO HOPS Chef Ben Hoyle from Sudbury, England, completed 75 successive pogo hops on the back wheel of his trail bike in September 2011.

BEER LABELS Since 1955, Charles Johnson of Cuyahoga Falls, Ohio, has collected more than 108,000 beer-bottle labels from all over the world.

500-MILE CRAWL In 2010, two Buddhist monks crawled 500 mi (800 km) on their knees to visit a statue in China's Putuo Mountains—a journey that took them two months.

SEVEN SUMMITS At just 16 years old, George Atkinson from London, England, reached the summit of the world's highest mountain, 29,029-ft (8,848-m) Mount Everest, and in doing so completed his challenge of conquering mountaineering's famous Seven Summits. Despite his young age, he had previously climbed Tanzania's Mount Kilimanjaro, Russia's Mount Elbrus, Indonesia's Carstensz Pyramid, Argentina's Mount Aconcagua, the United States' Mount McKinley, and Antarctica's Mount Vinson.

Ripley's ask

Ripley's Believe It or Not! met up with Erik Sprague to ask him about his extreme transformation.

Why did you decide to transform yourself into the Lizardman? Originally, I was working on ideas for body-based art pieces that explored transformation and how we use the term "human." This, combined with my interests in body modification and the sideshow, came together as a single project idea. I chose a lizard partly due to the cross-cultural symbolic significance of reptiles but also because I thought it would look good.

Do your modifications get a lot of attention from the public? Since the beginning my modifications have drawn a lot of attention, mostly double takes and staring, but over the years the attention has shifted from "What is that?" to "Hey, that's the guy from TV"—due in no small part to programs like Ripley's.

What is your favourite modification? My split tongue is the one I am most known for, but my favorite might be one that people rarely see—my septum piercing. The piercing is stretched to half an inch in diameter and I wear a small plug in it. It was done by a dear friend, Keith Alexander, who has since passed away and it has huge sentimental value to me.

Can you eat normally with your modified tongue and teeth? Yes, the only thing that has changed for me is that when I eat apples I no longer just bite into them because my sharp teeth simply tear off thin strips, so I have to slice them up first now.

Are you "completed" yet? I am not quite complete yet, with over 700 hours of tattooing on my body I still have about another 100 or so to go. Once all my scales are filled in green I will think of myself as complete, but that doesn't mean I won't come up with new additions in the future.

Turn the page

Lizardman

As a young boy

As Best Man

Wedding day

Performance artist Erik "The Lizardman" Sprague, from Austin, Texas, has spent years transforming himself into a reptile-man hybrid. Since 1994, he has undergone almost 700 hours of tattooing in order to achieve a full head and body of green scales. To complete his unique look, four of his teeth have been filed into sharp crocodile-like fangs, he has had his tongue bifurcated, and five Teflon horns have been subdermally implanted above each eye to form horned ridges. This last procedure was the most painful to endure—five hours with his head cut open, followed by swelling and soreness. He has also had his septum (the piece of skin that separates the nostrils) pierced and the hole stretched to ½ in (1.25 cm) in diameter.

During Erik's act, he inserts razor-sharp scissor blades in the fork of his tongue and through his nostrils, threads a metal corkscrew through his nose and mouth, and sticks a running power drill up his nostrils. He also swallows swords, eats and breathes fire, and acts as a human dartboard. On several occasions he pulled cars with his 1-in (2.5-cm) pierced earlobes, which at the time were the strongest earlobes in the world, but he had to stop wearing jewelry in them in 2009 following an adverse reaction.

Erik, who has a degree in Philosophy, estimates that it would cost around $250,000 for anyone wanting to achieve the same unbelievable look as The Lizardman.

The scissors carefully go right into his nasal passage!

He corkscrews through his nose, out of his mouth, and then through his ear!

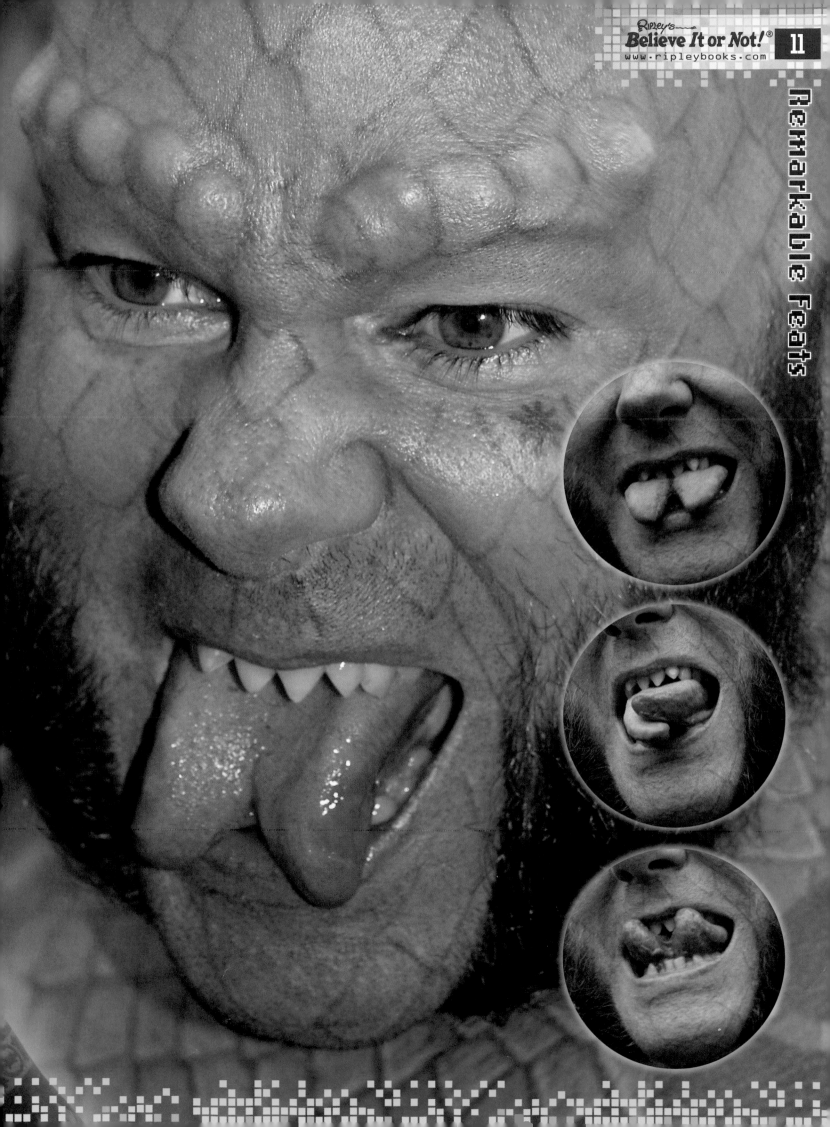

OVER 10,000 BEES!

BEE SUIT

In May 2011, Zhang Wei from Zizhou County, China, wore a suit of bees weighing a staggering 184 lb (83.5 kg)—that's approximately the weight of an adult American man. Wearing a pair of goggles, but leaving his face and hands unprotected and holding a tube in his mouth for breathing, he sat in a foliage-covered frame as thousands of bees were released next to him.

🅡 **ROCKET RACER** Students at the Joseph Leckie Community Technology College in Walsall, England, designed and developed a rocket-powered scale model car that reached a speed of 88.92 mph (143.1 km/h)—that's an equivalent speed of 259 mph (417 km/h) in a regular-sized car. The 21-in (53-cm) car was fitted with D-Class Estes rocket motors and fired 328 ft (100 m) along a high tensile wire.

🅡 **DELAYED GRADUATION** Leo Plass of Redmond, Oregon, dropped out of college in 1932 to take up a job in logging when he was less than one semester away from graduating—but in 2011 he finally received his diploma from Eastern Oregon University at the age of 99.

🅡 **LOTTA BOTTLES** Over a 25-year period, Steve Wheeler has collected more than 17,500 milk bottles in different shapes and sizes from around the world, some dating back to the 19th century. He has built a giant shed to house the collection, which weighs 15 tons, behind his home in Malvern, England. Ironically, Steve doesn't even like milk!

🅡 **SOCK LINE** As part of National Red Sock Day—in memory of yachtsman Sir Peter Blake who used to wear red socks for good luck—New Zealanders donated more than 30,000 socks, which, when stretched out on a line, extended for over 1.8 mi (3 km).

🅡 **WIRE BALL** Starting in 2001, landscaper Rick Fortin of New Boston, New Hampshire, has created a copper wire ball that now measures over 3 ft (0.9 m) in diameter and weighs more than 922 lb (418 kg).

DANCING BALLOON

Australian entertainer Bruce Airhead uses a voice-activated vacuum cleaner to inflate a 6-ft (1.8-m) balloon—and then he slides his entire body inside, bit by bit, and starts dancing. As a final twist, although he enters the balloon wearing only Lycra® shorts, he emerges through the burst balloon fully dressed as Elvis.

Ripley's Believe It or Not!®
www.ripleybooks.com
13
Remarkable Feats

Mass
Gathering Records

WHERE'S WALDO?

LARGE LEAF
On his way home from a park, nine-year-old Joseph Donato from Pickering, Canada, picked up a maple leaf that, without the stem, measured 13½ x 11½ in (34 x 29 cm)—that's bigger than most serving platters.

BIRD WATCH
British birdwatcher Chris Gooddie took just 12 months to find and photograph all 32 species of one of the world's most elusive birds, the pitta. He gave up a well-paid job as a sales director in London to travel 130,500 mi (210,000 km) around the world by plane, truck, motorbike, taxi, canoe, and motorboat to find the rare and secretive birds, which live in the rainforests of Africa, India, Southeast Asia, and Australia.

DAILY ASCENT
Matt Loughrey climbed Croagh Patrick, a 2,507-ft-high (764-m) mountain in County Mayo, Ireland, every day for a year between June 2010 and June 2011.

- **1,792 PEOPLE WEARING SANTA HATS** at Brockton, Massachusetts, on November 19, 2011.

- **8,734 PEOPLE DRESSED AS PIRATES** invaded Penzance in Cornwall, England, on June 26, 2011.

- **4,891 PEOPLE IN SMURF OUTFITS** in 11 countries across the world—including the United States, Mexico, and the U.K.—on June 25, 2011.

- **1,215 PEOPLE WEARING ROBIN HOOD COSTUMES** at Newark, Nottinghamshire, England, on August 28, 2011.

- **330 PEOPLE DRESSED AS ZOMBIES** broke the record for the most costumed riders on a theme park ride at Dorney Park & Wildwater Kingdom in Allentown, Pennsylvania, on August 18, 2011.

- **700 STUDENTS IN FROG MASKS** at Texas Tech, Lubbock, Texas, on April 29, 2011.

- **424 TEXAS RANGERS FANS WEAR SUNGLASSES IN THE DARK** —including former U.S. President George W. Bush—gathered at a night baseball game on June 21, 2011.

More than 3,500 people dressed in red-and-white striped costumes and black-rimmed spectacles assembled in a square in Dublin, Ireland, in June 2011 for a mass gathering of the Waldo character from the popular *Where's Waldo?* children's books. Some dogs even turned up dressed as Waldo.

SKYSCRAPER CLIMB

In a six-hour climb, Alain Robert, or "Spiderman," the French freestyle skyscraper climber, scaled the 2,717-ft-high (828-m) Burj Khalifa building in Dubai, United Arab Emirates, in March 2011. He has climbed over 70 of the world's tallest buildings, including New York's Empire State Building and Chicago's Willis Tower.

R WORLD WALK Jean Béliveau of Montréal, Canada, walked around the world for 11 years. He set off on his 45th birthday and traveled 46,940 mi (75,543 km) through 64 countries, wearing out 53 pairs of shoes on the longest-ever uninterrupted world walk. He ate insects in Africa, dog in South Korea, and snake in China, and carried his sleeping bag, clothes, and a first-aid kit in a three-wheel stroller.

R HAT MOSAIC The New Era Cap Company of Buffalo, New York State, created a hat mosaic made up of 1,875 official Major League Baseball caps.

R ICE ORDEAL Two Chinese men stood encased in ice for two hours in Zhangjiajie, Hunan Province, in 2011, wearing only their swimming trunks. Chen Kecai, 52, and Jin Songhao, 54, lasted 118 and 120 minutes respectively standing in transparent boxes with ice right up to their necks. Jin was even able to write Chinese calligraphy during the challenge.

R SENIOR WORKER Hedda Bolgar Bekker, who runs her own psychotherapy clinic in Los Angeles, California, still works at age 102, giving lectures and seeing patients for up to 20 hours a week.

Remarkable Feats

Willard Wigan

Willard Wigan, a sculptor from Birmingham, England, makes amazingly detailed microscopic sculptures. In 2011, Ripley's managed to acquire 97 pieces of his work to showcase in their museums. The Ripley's team spoke to Willard:

Ripley's **ask**

"I work in a closet 4 ft across to minimize air disturbance, and often at night when the vibrations from traffic are less. It's a messy space with bottles and tiny boxes containing ground diamond and glass, platinum, dust, those plastic clothes tags that I carve shapes into, cloth fibers, eyelashes, flies' hairs—all the materials I work with.

I can be in there for 20 hours or so at a time. I have trained myself to increase my concentration—when I started doing this sort of work 40 years ago I used to put tiny ball bearings at the ends of my fingers and hold them there for three hours. I would thread a needle 200 times to increase my attention span. I now find I can concentrate to such an extent that I enter a semi-meditative state.

I once wanted to carve a stately home small enough to fit in the eye of a needle and at about 3 p.m. one day I went into a U.K. grocery store and started looking in a magazine for inspiration. The next thing I knew, a sales assistant tapped me on the shoulder and said the store was closing. It was 5 p.m. and I had been staring at one picture for two hours! Another time, I was hollowing out a hair to make a space for a train I wanted to insert inside and held my breath—until I heard a loud bang. That was the sound of me hitting the floor. I'd held my breath too long and passed out.

After concentrating for a few hours, my movements are slow for a while when I stop. I have to train myself to see again that some things are big and don't need such a gentle touch. I don't enjoy doing my work because it's so demanding, but I love finishing a sculpture and seeing people's reaction to it.

If I'm making something to fit in the eye of a needle, I'll carve the sculpture outside the needle first. I have to watch out for the catapult action. I have a clamp that holds the model and if I press too hard it'll catapult off, or static electricity might make it jump. I made a whole scene of Miss Haversham, Estella, and Pip, from Great Expectations, complete with cobwebs and cakes, but it catapulted away. That was three months' work lost. I was pretty upset. Another time, a bead of sweat ran down my fingers onto a wet sculpture as I painted it and entombed it. Ruined. And sometimes I might inhale work, as I did once with Alice in Wonderland.

After that, if the model has, say, two legs, I drill two tiny holes in the needle and fill the holes with honey. I drop the feet in and surface tension holds the model enough for me to paint it, after which it hardens. I've dropped sculptures on the floor before and people shriek and panic that it's broken, but it never does. If an ant falls off your house roof, it won't die. It's too small. A speck of dust on your shirt will still be there even if you jump up and down. Same with the models.

Paint has to be worked on before I can use it because the pigment molecules in it can be too big for the sculptures. I drop a speck of paint on a microscope slide and grind down the molecules with a ball bearing for two to three hours until the paint becomes smoother. There's no second chance with the painting. You can't wipe it off and start again.

My aim is to create smaller and smaller artworks. My next project will be to capture the "Old Woman Who Lived in a Shoe," complete with 25 children and the shoe... in the eye of a needle!

I think I draw people's attention to the wonder of the minuscule world. After all, everything starts small—even us, as a tiny speck in the womb. Microscopic bacteria can cause massive devastation and survive against the odds. An atom might be one of the smallest things that exists, but it produces the biggest explosion."

TO VIEW THE COLLECTION

Turn the page

R **HAIRCUT TOUR** Hair salon owner Patrick Lomantini from Wichita, Kansas, did at least 50 free haircuts a day, in all 50 U.S. states in 50 days in 2011—a total of more than 2,500 haircuts. Visiting a different state each day, he traveled between states overnight and cut hair all day.

R **SWALLOWED SAW** On November 14, 2010, U.S. sword swallower Dan Meyer swallowed a 100-year-old handsaw, which belonged to the Bruce Museum in Greenwich, Connecticut, during a presentation on the history of sword swallowing.

Willard Wigan, a sculptor from Birmingham, England, makes amazingly detailed microscopic sculptures, some of which measure just 0.0002 in (0.005 mm) tall—more than three times smaller than the period at the end of this sentence. His figures can be viewed only under a microscope and magnified 400 times. They can fit on a single grain of sand or on the head of a pin, and he has even managed to fit nine camels into the eye of a needle.

Now, 97 of his stunning miniature artworks have been bought by *Ripley's Believe It or Not!*—and most of them, the result of more than 40 years of painstaking carving, chipping, and painting, could fit comfortably together inside a single matchbox.

As a child with undiagnosed dyslexia, Willard had an unhappy time at school and sought refuge in local woods, where he watched ants running about the floor of a shed. "I was four or five," he recalls, "and I thought the ants must be homeless, so I built them houses from splinters of wood. Then I thought the ants needed furniture, so I made little chairs and tables that could fit inside the houses." His mother saw the ant houses and encouraged him to continue. "She told me that I was going to get bigger by getting smaller."

Each nano-sculpture takes up to three months to create. His homemade carving tools consist of tiny shards of diamond attached to a needle, as well as filed-down acupuncture needles. He uses one of his own eyelashes or a hair plucked from the back of a housefly as a paintbrush. To keep his hands still, he enters a meditative state and works in the 1.5-second space between heartbeats, as even the pulse in his finger is enough to cause a mistake.

His stunningly accurate creations include Little Miss Muffet, with spider, in the eye of a needle, Muhammad Ali boxing Sonny Liston on a pinhead, the Statue of Liberty in the eye of a needle, the *Titanic* on a tiny crystal, a church on a grain of sand, and the cast of *Peter Pan* in a fishhook. His work is mentally and physically draining, but he strives to get smaller still. Referring to the nine camels in the eye of a needle, he says: "One day, I'll get 20 in there. It'll probably drive me nuts, but I will do it."

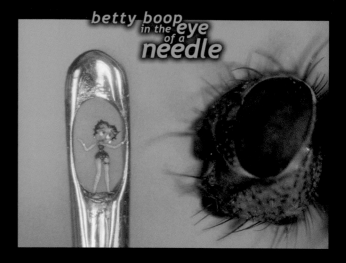

betty boop in the **eye** of a **needle**

nine camels in the **eye** of a **needle**

I had to look through the microscope several times to check my eyes weren't deceiving me

~

Lord Richard Rogers

statue of *liberty* in the **eye** of a **needle**

ali vs. *liston* on the **head** of a **pin**

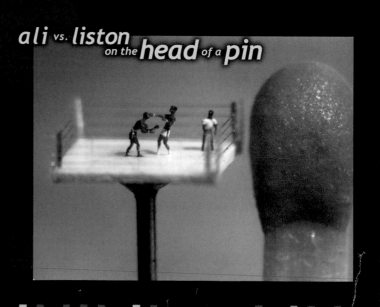

titanic on the **tip** of a **crystal**

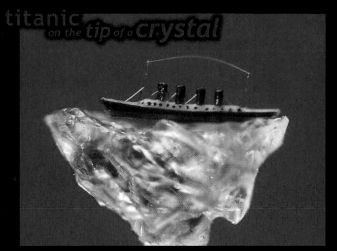

Ripley's archivist Edward Meyer tells how he acquired the collection

"I had been following Willard Wigan's career since 1999, and when he first sold some of his artworks in 2007 and a website listed several for sale, I realized that maybe Ripley's could obtain a couple. Following dozens of letters and a meeting in a London hotel bar, I decided to try and buy a large number of his works. During negotiations the figure rose to 97 pieces—which was everything not already in private collections or about 85–90 percent of everything he has ever made. The art was delivered by hand in a gym bag to our Orlando HQ, all contained in small jewelry cases inside three small cardboard boxes."

I spy with my little eye...

little miss muffet in the **eye** of a **needle**

rugby player on **pinhead** scoring goal through **eye of needle**

Willard's talents defy description

~

H.R.H. Prince Charles

hairy biker on the **head** of a **pin**

GOLF HANDICAP

Carbrook Golf Club in Brisbane, Australia, has some unique obstacles on its course—sharks. A dozen or so bull sharks circle the waters in the lake alongside the 12th to 15th tees, their fins poking through the water proving a distraction for even the most hardened pro. The 9-ft-long (2.7-m), 330-lb (150-kg) man-eaters spilled into the lake in the mid-1990s during a flood from nearby rivers that source in coastal Moreton Bay, some 5 mi (8 km) away—and have happily since bred in the lake's waters.

R EASY CATCH Jason Kresse of Freeport, Texas, was out fishing for red snapper in the Gulf of Mexico in March 2011 when a 375-lb (170-kg) mako shark leaped into his boat without provocation, thrashing about and damaging the vessel before dying hours later.

R PIER PRESSURE Harnessing winds of more than 60 mph (96 km/h) on November 11, 2010, kiteboarder Lewis Crathern of Worthing, England, became the first person to jump clean over Brighton Pier. He navigated the waves for about two hours before finally finding one big enough to launch him on his death-defying leap over the 50-ft-high (15-m) pier.

R TIED FINISH Five runners—Brad Weiss, Chris Solarz, Terence Gerchberg, Stephen England, and Francis Laros—finished the 2011 God's Country Marathon in Coudersport, Pennsylvania, in 3 hours 26 minutes—while tethered together.

R KITEBOARD CROSSING Russian extreme sport enthusiasts Yevgeny Novozheev and Konstantin Aksyonov became the first people to cross the 60-mi (97-km) Bering Strait from Russia to Alaska by kiteboard. During their seven-hour journey, they survived water temperatures of 34°F (1°C), a fierce storm, and a collision with a whale.

R DOUBLE ACE Golfer Adam Smith from Aberdeenshire, Scotland, beat odds of 67 million to one by getting two holes-in-one in the space of seven holes during a round of golf at nearby Stonehaven in January 2011.

R EXTRA LARGE Former Welsh international soccer player Robbie Savage managed to wear soccer shirts from all 72 English Football League clubs at the same time.

Monster Wave

On November 1, 2011, American surfer Garrett McNamara set a new world record by riding a 90-ft (27-m) wave off the coast of Portugal. Towed by Jet Ski out to the freak swell, which was created by a 1,000-ft-deep (300-m) underwater canyon in the area, he managed to catch a lift on a moving wall of water, which was the height of a nine-story building.

Remarkable Feats

R **IRON MAN** Seventy-year-old pastor Bob Kurtz—known as "Golf's Iron Man"—completed 1,850 holes of golf over a seven-day period at Quail Creek Golf Resort, Hartselle, Alabama, in June 2011. Despite playing for 16 hours a day in temperatures touching 100°F (38°C), he still shot an average score of just 74 (par for the course is 72), and shot better than his age four times.

R **PUNTER'S JOY** In March 2011, Steve Whiteley from Devon, England, used his bus pass to get to Exeter racecourse for free, entered for free through a promotion, and then proceeded to win more than £1.4 million from a £2 bet. The 61-year-old heating engineer, who goes to the races only twice a year, backed the winning horse in all six races at total odds of 879,138 to one. Making his wager all the more remarkable, Jessica Lodge, the victorious jockey in the last race, had never previously ridden a winner.

R **ENDURANCE RACE** The 2011 Hoka Hey Motorcycle Challenge traveled through 48 U.S. states and part of Canada, from Mesa, Arizona, to Sydney, Nova Scotia—a journey of over 14,000 mi (22,530 km). Entry is limited to Harley-Davidson bikers, and during the event riders must never sleep more than 10 ft (3 m) away from their bike, which rules out nights in hotels. The race was won for the second successive year by Florida's Will Barclay, who completed the course in just two weeks.

R **HIGH BASKET** From the top of a light tower that was almost 220 ft (67 m) above the ground, basketball stunt team How Ridiculous (comprising Derek Herron, Brett Stanford, Scott Gaunson, and Kyle Nebel) sank an incredible basket at the Western Australia Cricket Association Ground in Perth in 2011.

R **UNBROKEN RUN** From 1992 to 2010, National Football League quarterback Brett Favre started in 297 consecutive games.

R **BRAVE SWIMMER** Despite losing nearly half his body in China's 2008 Sichuan earthquake, Dai Guohong has become one of his country's top swimmers. He lost both legs when they were crushed under tons of rubble after the roof of his Beichuan school collapsed, killing 26 of his classmates.

NEAR MISS

This is the moment when Raimana van Bastolaer nearly lost his head to a flying Jet Ski during a surfing contest in his native Tahiti. As the waves in the region are so big, surfers are towed out by Jet Ski, but Van Bastolaer's friend, Reef McIntosh, lost control of the machine, which was pulled over the lip of the 12-ft (3.6-m) wave, missing the surfer's head by inches.

ON JULY 2, 2011, A WORLD-RECORD 272 BODYBOARDERS GATHERED IN THE WATER SIMULTANEOUSLY AT FIGUEIRA DA FOZ, PORTUGAL.

Remember the *Addams Family* house? Well, it looks mundane and suburban compared to Steve Bard's rambling Victorian home in Seattle, Washington, where every room is crammed from floor to ceiling with hundreds of thousands of curiosities, ranging from an 8-ft-tall (2.4-m) human skeleton to two-headed animals and a collection of 100-year-old pickled human fetuses in jars.

Known as "Weird Steve," Bard is in fact just an average guy with a passion for collecting things—the stranger the better. That's why he is happy to share his home with funeral ephemera, monster movie props, sci-fi art, questionable medical devices, weird taxidermy, Victorian hair art, countless skulls, and the world's smallest mummy.

A self-confessed sci-fi geek, he started out collecting books, but as he picked up oddities and old sideshow artifacts on eBay and from various other sources, his collection spread out from the library to fill the entire house and garden. He has over 25,000 books (including thousands of autographed sci-fi first editions), more than 150 antique toasters, plus a collection of casket plates, antique funeral caskets, and embalmer and mortician tools.

Then there are the animals. While live birds reside in the kitchen, everything else is dead. There are stuffed gazelles, bears, monkeys, and a tiger, as well as preserved curiosities such as conjoined weasels, two-headed kittens, two-headed chicks, and a two-headed calf. Many of his exhibits are stored in jars, including a pickled bat, a giant tapeworm, and a jar containing a human finger lost in an accident in the 1950s. Among Steve's most prized possessions are his "pickled punks"—Victorian human fetuses preserved in formaldehyde that were once sideshow attractions. They were known as "frog babies" because they were stillborn with anencephaly, a disorder whereby most of the brain is missing owing to a neural tube defect. Steve keeps these in jars on the mantle above his bed!

However, not everything in the house is as it seems. The giant human skeleton is thought to have been made for medical students, while a two-headed baby is actually made of rubber. Steve had to create it himself because, as he acknowledges, it is not easy to obtain real two-headed babies.

Paintings line every wall of the house, and Steve also has hundreds of kinetic art objects and art deco statues. His more unusual artistic exhibits include a series of paintings on the head of a pin and Victorian art woven from human hair.

Adjoining the library is a "Devil Room" devoted to all things Satanic, and the basement has been converted to a glow-in-the-dark "Future Room," decorated in the style of *The Jetsons* and *Barbarella*, and containing futuristic furniture in the form of an egg-shaped stereo chair as well as a sensory-deprivation tank.

This shrine of creepy curiosities extends outside, where Steve has set up a Minotaur Garden in his backyard. The garden features a 14-ft-high (4-m) bust of a Minotaur, a 25-ft-tall (7.6-m) Rapunzel Castle Tower, and a sinister cemetery. For all the weirdness that surrounds him, Steve claims the weirdest thing of all was the one question that a lady visitor to his house wanted to ask: "How do you dust?"

Every inch of Steve Bard's house is filled with old sideshow artifacts and weird human and animal curiosities. The narrow paths that wind from room to room are just wide enough for a person to walk through. Yet it remains a functional house. The kitchen boasts a microwave, a refrigerator, and a burner, all cleverly concealed by human skulls, figures, severed heads, and other oddities. The house is not open to the general public, but Steve does sometimes give private tours to those who share his eclectic taste in the freaky and the creepy.

WEIRDEST OF THE WEIRD

Darryl Learie of Alberta, Canada, is able to complete one-armed push-ups on the top of a raw egg, without smashing it. Incredibly, Darryl's record stands at 11 repetitions before the egg finally gave way. Darryl explains that the arched top and bottom of the shell enable the egg to withstand the forces he exerts when performing the feat.

EGGSERCISE!

REAL EGG!

CHIN UP

Farmer Zhu Baobing is capable of carrying great weights on his chin. Known locally in Guli, China, as "China's First Chin," he successfully held aloft a 90-lb (40-kg) child while filming a TV program in Jiangsu Province in May 2011.

R HOT WHEELS Driving down a ramp ten stories high and designed to look like a Hot Wheels toy ramp, Hollywood stuntman Tanner Foust jumped his car across a world-record-breaking 332-ft (101-m) gap before the running of the Indianapolis 500 in May 2011.

R DUCK LINE Families from Seattle, Washington State, joined forces to create a record-breaking line of 17,782 yellow rubber ducks that stretched a mile long at the city's Warren G. Magnuson Park.

R CHOPSTICK CHAMP Ma Deqi, a farmer from Yuzhou, China, can catch 40 Ping Pong balls with a pair of chopsticks in one minute.

R TWO-DAY KISS Husband and wife Ekkachai and Laksana Tiranarat kissed nonstop for 46 hours 24 minutes to celebrate Valentine's Day in Pattaya, Thailand, in 2011.

R BLOWING BUBBLES In 2011, British professional bubble-maker Samsam Bubbleman (real name Sam Heath) created a large bubble, 19 in (48 cm) in diameter, with 56 smaller bubbles inside. It took him over two hours to blow and required conditions of low wind, low humidity, and no rain. He has been making amazing bubbles since 1989, and once managed to fit 50 people inside a giant bubble.

STILT WALK Wearing specially made 2-ft-high (60-cm) aluminum stilts, Samati Yiming, a 33-year-old physics teacher, walked 65 ft (20 m) on a high wire that was suspended 70 ft (21 m) above the ground at a park in Xinjiang, China. Samati, who has been stilt walking for over 15 years, did not even use a safety rope. In 2004, he walked for eight days on stilts, covering 180 mi (290 km), and the following year he walked for 49 steps on stilts that were an incredible 52 ft (16 m) high.

MOUNTAIN WALK In 2009, 34-year-old Buddhist monk Endo Mitsunaga completed the "Sennichi Kaihogyo"—one thousand days of meditation and walking around Mount Hiei, Japan. During this time he walked 26 mi (42 km) a day, for periods of 100 or 200 days in a row.

EYE RUN Noel Bresland from Manchester, England, ran 26 mi (42 km)—the equivalent of a marathon—on a treadmill inside a capsule of the giant wheel, the London Eye, in 3 hours 51 minutes in London, England, in April 2011.

EXTRA LARGE In June 2011 in Nashville, Tennessee, a manufacturer unveiled a colossal T-shirt measuring 180 x 281 ft (54.8 x 85.6 m)—that's nearly the size of a football field. The T-shirt took six weeks to make and weighed more than two tons.

SCISSOR HAPPY Barber Nabi Salehi of London, England, cut the hair of 526 customers in just 24 hours on June 3, 2011.

STUNNING STOGIE In 2011, Cuba's José Castelar "Cueto" Cairo rolled a massive cigar that measured over 268 ft (81.8 m) long.

MAGIC NUMBER Indian businessman Mohammed Farooque Dhanani from Mumbai, has collected more than 31,000 currency notes from across the world—all ending with the serial number 786. The number has no particular significance—he simply started collecting it over a decade ago as a unique hobby. His biggest surprise since then was finding that the serial number on his new credit card ended in 786.

OPTICAL EXTRUSION

Kung fu expert Dong Changsheng performed an incredible feat at a festival in Hubei Province, China. Reports claim that he swallowed two metal ball bearings, before executing several martial arts moves to move the balls up into the back of his mouth. He then proceeded to force the balls out of one of his eyes, with the help of a chopstick!

Ripley's Research

Dong claims he is able to propel the small metal balls through the narrow tunnels in his head, eventually maneuvering them out of his eyes through the tear ducts. Dong explains "The tear ducts actually connect to other tunnels in the head, and normal people just haven't broken the barrier and made the connection through." At 50 years old, he has been stretching the limits of his eyes for at least 15 years. He began by placing buttons in his eyes to toughen them up, and is now capable of many eye-watering endeavors: Dong was featured in Ripley's Believe It or Not! Seeing is Believing after pulling a minibus attached to hooks under his eyelids.

Granny's Six-pack

At 75, grandmother Ernestine Shepherd of Baltimore, Maryland, is the world's oldest competitive female bodybuilder. She wakes up at 3 a.m. every day to meditate, and then clocks up runs totaling 10 mi (16 km) before lunch. She started working out when she reached the age of 56, but has since won two bodybuilding contests and run nine marathons.

Have you always been into fitness and health? I didn't get into the fitness and health industry until I was 56, when my sister and I were invited to a church picnic, and they told us we could wear bathing suits. We put our bathing suits on and she said: "Wow, we don't look good, we need to do something." She was 57 and I was 56—we started exercising and noticed the change in our bodies, and we loved it!

You started an online fitness program in 2006 at the age of 71—tell us how things developed from there. I had always wanted to become a bodybuilder, but I didn't know how to go about it. I was introduced to trainer and former Mr. Universe, Yohnnie Shambourger and he developed a special training program for me. Over the next seven months my body made an incredible transformation and I was ready to compete against women half my age.

How does it feel to hold the world record? It feels great, because so many people have come to me and said: "Wow! How did you do that?" Just to have people ask me that question is wonderful to me.

Tell us what your daily routine consists of? I wake up every morning, at 3 a.m. Then I have my devotions, eat my breakfast, get dressed, and I am out that door getting ready to run. When I get back, I eat breakfast again and prepare to go to the gym. I have classes that I train in during the day, so I am at the gym until maybe about 8 or 9 o'clock at night. But I come home in between and rest.

Do you have a specific diet to accompany your routine? I have a very strict diet that I have been following for about ten years—without cheating! First thing in the morning I eat a banana, then I go out and run and drink water. When I get back, I eat four boiled eggs—one with the yolk in it and the other three without. Then, I will have crushed pineapples. I also eat a lot of chicken, tuna fish, turkey, frozen vegetables, brown rice, white potato, and sweet potato. My most important drink is liquid egg whites four or five times a day.

What is your motto for a healthy life? My motto for a healthy life would be to remember that you need to strength train each day, do at least one hour's worth of cardio, drink plenty of water, and of course five to six small meals a day. That's how I do it, and that's how I have stayed healthy.

⭐ FITNESS FANATIC At 102 years old, former postman Shi Xiaochun of Xiaoshan, China, still worked out every day, doing pushups on his fists and even on one hand.

⭐ LONGEST JUMP On July 2, 2011, Algerian-born Taig Khris set a new world record for the longest jump on rollerblades when he leaped 95 ft (29 m) in front of the Sacre Coeur Basilica in Paris, France.

⭐ KUNG FU GRANNY Zhao Yufang, an 82-year-old grandmother from Beijing, China, is a master in Shaolin kung fu. She had wanted to learn kung fu as a girl, but her local master would not teach her. So she taught herself, went back to the school, and defeated the master, forcing him to apologize.

⭐ FOOTBALL ON WHEELS Founded in 2008 in San Marcos, Texas, the Unicycle Football League features teams playing American football while balancing atop unicycles. Players wear bike helmets but no shoulder pads.

⭐ SUMO RUNNER Weighing in at 400 lb (180 kg), American sumo wrestler Kelly Gneiting became the heaviest man ever to complete a marathon when he finished the 2011 Los Angeles Marathon in 9 hours 48 minutes 52 seconds. Battling heavy rain and strong winds, he jogged the first 8 mi (12.9 km) and walked the last 18 mi (29 km).

⭐ CHEESE REMEDY Nursing a badly bruised shin that left her participation in the 2010 Winter Olympics in Vancouver in doubt, U.S. alpine skier Lindsey Vonn tried cream and painkillers to no effect before deciding to smear the wound with soft cheese. The cheesy remedy was so successful that a few days later she won gold in the downhill event.

⭐ 10TH DAN Standing only 4 ft 10 in (1.47 m) tall and weighing just 100 lb (45.4 kg), Sensei Keiko Fukuda of San Francisco, California, became the first woman in history to reach the highest rank of 10th dan black belt in judo. Only three other living judokas have reached that level—and they're all men. She became a judo instructor in 1937, and in 2011 was still teaching judo three times a week—at age 98.

⭐ JET-SKI RECORD Reaching top speeds in excess of 69 mph (110 km/h), Jeremy Burfoot of Auckland, New Zealand, covered a world record 1,421 mi (2,287 km) on a Jet Ski in 24 hours on Lake Karapiro on February 8, 2011.

VOLCANO BOARDING

Guests at a hostel in León, Nicaragua, can hike to the top of the Cerro Negro volcano and then board down 1,640 ft (500 m) of its steep slopes at speeds of more than 50 mph (80 km/h). Formed in 1850, the Cerro Negro ("black mountain") is Central America's youngest volcano and also one of its most active, having already erupted 20 times.

⭐ CHESS CHALLENGE Israeli grandmaster Alik Gershon played 523 games of chess simultaneously in Tel Aviv on October 21, 2010—and defeated 454 of his opponents.

⭐ ARMLESS PITCHER Born without arms, Tom Willis from San Diego, California, has thrown out the ceremonial first pitch at more than a dozen Major League baseball games. He throws the ball with his right foot, and his pitches usually make the entire distance from the mound to home plate (60 ft 6 in/18.4 m) without bouncing.

SPEARED FOOT

Track and field judge Lia Marie Lourenco receives medical aid after a competitor's javelin speared her foot during the warm up for the Troféu Brasil championship in São Paulo. She was rushed to hospital, where she underwent surgery to remove the javelin tip.

Nailed It!

Xu Tiancheng can do a headstand on a nail for 30 minutes—and he has the dent in the top of his head to prove it! The 56-year-old performs his unusual ritual as part of his daily morning exercise routine at a park in Changsha, China—a pain-defying display of endurance that attracts large crowds.

PLANE SWAP

In an incredible midair stunt, Austrian skydiver Paul Steiner climbed from one glider to another 6,560 ft (2,000 m) up in the air while both planes were traveling at 100 mph (160 km/h). He climbed out of the cockpit, crawled along the wing, somersaulted under the wing, and then stepped onto the wing of the second glider flying below. Then, while the first glider turned upside down and flew overhead, Steiner reached up to form a human link between the two planes.

Steiner sits on the wing of the first glider

KNIFE EXERCISE Xie Guanghai, a 57-year-old physics professor in Luoyang, China, does 4,000 push-ups a day—on upturned chopping knives. By developing thick calluses on his palms, he feels no pain from the blades of the knives, which are held in place on a wooden board.

BUNNY HOPS Polish stunt cyclist Krystian Herba bunny-hopped his way up the 48 flights of the 656-ft-high (200-m) Millennium Tower in Vienna, Austria, in 18 minutes 9 seconds.

BUNGEE JUMPS Scott Huntly from Edinburgh, Scotland, made 107 bungee jumps in just nine hours from a bridge 702 ft (214 m) above the Bloukrans River in the Western Cape region of South Africa.

THE CZECH TECHNICAL UNIVERSITY HAS DESIGNED A ROBOT THAT CAN JUGGLE FIVE POOL BALLS AT ONCE.

CROSSING AMERICA In 2010, six British and U.S. servicemen ran 3,530 mi (5,648 km) from New York to Santa Monica, California, on a Gumpathon, named after the movie *Forrest Gump* in which the hero runs across the United States. Their eight-week journey took them through three deserts, four time zones, ten mountain ranges, 16 states, and 789 towns. Among the team, which ran in relays, was British Royal Marine Mark Ormrod, a triple amputee who lost both legs and one arm when he stepped on a land mine in Afghanistan on Christmas Eve 2007.

SENIOR SKYDIVER In March 2011, Fred Mack of Newtown Square, Pennsylvania, celebrated his 100th birthday by performing a tandem skydive at an altitude of 13,000 ft (3,960 m) in the skies over New Jersey. He made his first skydiving jump aged 95 and vowed to repeat the feat if he lived to be 100.

YO-YO HERO James Buffington, founder of the Chicago Yo-Yo Club, has built a working yo-yo with a string length of 39 ft 9 in (12.1 m). He demonstrated it from the roof of a store in the city, where it hung down over three stories.

POLE POSITION Israeli stuntman Hezi Dean stood on a small platform on top of a nine-story-high pole in Tel Aviv for more than 35 hours in May 2011. A crane hoisted him to the top of the pole and he descended at the end of the endurance test by jumping into a pile of cardboard boxes.

CAREFUL CLIMB In December 2010, the Czech Republic's Anatol Stykan climbed the 235 steps leading up to the famous Sacre Coeur church in Paris, France, while balancing his partner Monika on his head.

Ripley's REVISITED
Joel Wahl

YOUR UPLOADS
www.ripleys.com/submit

Benji Williams

Benji Williams of Los Angeles, California, has been making rubber-band balls since he was six. He went to Orlando, Florida, on vacation to visit Ripley's warehouse to see the world's biggest rubber-band ball, made by Joel Waul and weighing 9,432 lb (4,282 kg). Benji's ball is already well over 100 lb (45 kg)—and growing fast.

UNDERWATER CARD GAME A group of 16 German scuba divers played a card game underwater for 36 hours in March 2011. The divers sat on the bottom of a pool in Geiselhoering, playing a traditional Bavarian card game called "Sheep's Head."

STAR SWIMMER Four-year-old Tae Smith from Poole, England, swam 101 lengths of a pool (1¼ mi/2,000 m) just five months after learning to swim. She was meant to swim 30 lengths, but kept going until she had swum more than triple the distance.

He somersaults under the wing

Standing on the fuselage of the second glider, he stretches up to grab the first plane

HARD TO SWALLOW

Liang Yuxin from Xia Mei, China, can regurgitate live goldfish, coins, and even a 50-in-long (127-cm) chain. He discovered his unusual talent as a boy after accidentally swallowing a ball and finding that he could bring it back up at will.

OLDEST RANGER Betty Reid Soskin is still an active ranger in the U.S. National Park Service—at the age of 90. She works at Rosie the Riveter National Historic Park in Richmond, California, six hours a day, five days a week.

FLAMINGO FAN Sherry Knight of Lecanto, Florida, loves flamingos so much that years ago she started collecting flamingo-related items—and now has over 619 pieces of flamingo memorabilia.

LOST LEG A year after losing his right leg in a climbing accident, Hungarian climber Zsolt Eross scaled the world's fourth-highest mountain—the 27,940-ft (8,516-m) peak of Lhotse in the Himalayas—wearing his replacement prosthetic leg.

ROUTE 66 Andy McMenemy from Harrogate, England, ran 66 ultramarathons—each 31 mi (50 km) long—on 66 consecutive days in 66 different cities in the U.K.

ROCK STAR Alex Honnold of Sacramento, California, climbs some of the most daunting cliff faces in the world—without a safety rope. The free-climber scaled the notorious 2,000-ft (610-m) northwest face of the Half Dome in Yosemite National Park, California, solo in only 2 hours 50 minutes—an ascent that can take some climbers up to five days.

LOOSE CHANGE Craig Davidson of Phoenix, Arizona, collects loose change he finds as he takes his morning jogs. In 30 years, he has found more than $8,400 in dropped coins.

POLAR FIRST Taking advantage of seasonal melting ice caps in August 2011, a team of six British explorers—Jock Wishart, David Mans, Billy Gammon, Mark Delstanche, Mark Beaumont, and Rob Sleep—became the first people to row to the magnetic North Pole. During their 450-mi (720-km), month-long voyage through Arctic waters, they encountered polar bears, collided with icebergs, and Wishart was bitten by a seal.

GUM COLLECTOR Sarah Maughan of Idaho Falls, Idaho, has collected over 1,400 different packages of gum. She began collecting gum in 1948, beginning with a pack of Popeye bubble gum, and has been adding new types and flavors for more than 60 years.

SCUBA DIVE Diver and scuba instructor Allen Sherrod of Groveland, Florida, spent more than five days 20 ft (6 m) underwater in Lake David to complete the longest ever freshwater dive. He surfaced on September 16, 2011, after 120 hours 14 minutes 32 seconds in the lake, during which time he entertained himself with a waterproof keyboard and monitor that enabled him to watch movies and check Facebook.

EPIC FLIGHT Paraplegic pilot Dave Sykes of Dewsbury, England, flew an ultralight aircraft 13,480 mi (21,700 km) from the U.K. to Sydney, Australia. Sykes, who lost the use of his legs in a motorbike accident in 1993, battled through dust storms, thunder and lightning, and baking heat on his three-month solo flight over 20 countries.

Ripley's Believe It or Not!®
www.ripleybooks.com
33
Remarkable Feats

MOUNTAIN JUMP In September 2011, stuntman Jeb Corliss of Malibu, California, flew from the 5,000-ft-high (1,524-m) summit of China's Tianmen Mountain wearing a wingsuit—which has extra fabric between the legs and under the arms to help with lift. He glided like a bird down the mountain and across surrounding valleys before landing safely by parachute on a mountain road.

ONE-TRACK MIND A collector of rare vintage toy trains for 50 years, Jerry Greene amassed over 35,000 items, worth a total of more than $50 million. He kept them in the basement of his home in Philadelphia, Pennsylvania. He had about 1,700 locomotives and cars, 700 stations, and thousands of accessories. When he decided to sell the collection, it took his family three weeks to unpack just 5,000 of the pieces for display.

LIVING WITH LIONS Ukrainian private zoo owner Alexander Pylyshenko lived for 36 days in a cage with a lioness and her two cubs. He slept on hay on the floor and ate food that was passed through the bars. He installed a toilet and shower inside the cage for personal hygiene, but had to avoid using shampoos and deodorants in case they irritated the lions. An artist by profession, he spent much of his time in the cage painting portraits of his roommates.

GOLD COIN Australia's Perth Mint unveiled the world's largest gold coin in 2011, weighing 2,205 lb (1,000 kg) and measuring 31½ in (80 cm) in diameter and more than 4¾ in (12 cm) thick. Made of 99.99 percent pure gold, the supersized coin bears an image of Queen Elizabeth II on one side and a leaping kangaroo on the other, and is worth more than $50 million.

DOUBLE MUSCLE

Strongman pastor Kevin Fast enlisted the help of his 18-year-old son Jacob to pull two fire trucks 100 ft (30 m) down the street in their hometown of Cobourg, Ontario, in June 2011. Combined, the trucks weighed a massive 153,780 lb (69,755 kg). The event was the latest in a long line of strength feats for Kevin. He has also pulled an entire house and a giant CC-177 Globemaster III airplane weighing 208 tons.

Index

ACKNOWLEDGMENTS

6–7 Courtesy of Food For Louis; 8 (t) Dinesh Upadhyaya, (b) © Jörg Mitter/Red Bull Content Pool; 10 (t/l) Erik Sprague; 12 (t/l, t/r) Quirky China News/Rex Features; 12–13 (b) Bruce Airhead; 13 (t) Barbara Lindberg/Rex Features; 14 Sipa Press/Rex Features; 15 (t) Willard Wigan Ltd; 20–25 Bradford Bohonus; 26 (l) © Photoshot, (r) Darryl Learie; 27 Quirky China News/Rex Features; 29 (t/r, c/r, b/r) Bigfoot Hostel, Nicaragua, (b) Reuters/Jonne Roriz-Agencia Estado; 30 (b) © Europics, (l, r) Quirky China News/Rex Features; 31 (t/l, c/l) Courtesy of Katalin Williams, (b/l, b/r) © Europics; 32 © Europics; **Back cover** Dinesh Upadhyaya

Key: t = top, b = bottom, c = center, l = left, r = right, sp = single page, dp = double page

All other photos are from Ripley Entertainment Inc.
Every attempt has been made to acknowledge correctly and contact copyright holders and we apologize in advance
for any unintentional errors or omissions, which will be corrected in future editions.